WORD STRINGS

PEARLS OF WISDOM FOR EVERYONE

VOLUME 1

ANN-MARIE ADAMS

ISBN: 978-1-4834-6961-4 (sc)
ISBN: 978-1-4834-6962-1 (e)

Library of Congress Control Number: 2017908115

Lulu Publishing Services rev. date: 08/29/2017

To Cooks Valley
…where the cows signal the end of the day and the
overnight train whistle sends you to slumber.

Contents

Foreword

The Word Strings project started as a personal challenge to construct words into meaningful narrative phrases for a blog series. Soon after, friends and family began requesting custom works for special occasions, followed by inserting phrases into song lyrics for Americana music. The strings are emotive and illustrative but lean toward inspirational prose. Read them to wrap words around life events.
Insert them when finding the right words to say is important.
Post and share them when it makes a difference.

Acknowledgments

Much appreciation to the Lowcountry Women Writers group in Beaufort, South Carolina, for their patience, wisdom, and humor. Thank you for listening to the duds with as much enthusiasm as you did for the strings that made it to print.

A resounding applause goes out to Katie McWhorter, Jessie Walker and Bridget Strawn for their youthful exuberance and abundance of talent to launch the *Word Strings Project* in the online arena. Presence counts for everything.

Logo and monogram credit: Katie McWhorter.

PART 1

TRANSITION

Affection

Affection is often directed toward others, but if it were to first flow inward, it would create an amazing life space to which many would find themselves bound.

Aging

Our humanness is more apparent as we age.

Fill the gaps and widen the circumference.
Make each step count is the mantra.

While change is inevitable, the means
to remain fulfilled stands still.

Benchmark

You are the only benchmark in life that you need. The time one spends on a bench is just as purposeful as setting sights on the next destination.

Birthday

In each and every way, you radiate.
Today is just a beacon to what will no
doubt evolve into an unforgettable life.

Breathing

Breathe in what makes you stronger.
Breathe out what no longer supports breathing in.

Chances

However long life may be, there are moments when
second chances find a way around the bend.

The matter is no longer about what to do.
Rather embrace what passes by for what it brings.
Recognize it as a familiar heartbeat, link, or view.

Much of life's journey isn't bound to
remain on the path but instead becomes
the compass to what lies ahead.

Change

Change, no matter how abrupt or affronting, can bring humanity to a place where all the sorrows of yesterday find hope in today.

Chord

Pull the chord that inspires you.
It is what strikes the bell to toll.

The unbridled effort reverberates, unleashing sound.

What is evident for all unfolds as
often as the bell rings.

Comeback

The common denominator of resilience and reinvention is the recognition that what transpires in one's life is significant but not defining.

Conserve

Every day with a little less, more is possible.

Know that every day is new, each experience
is rich, and no matter the hour you live in,
there's a tomorrow that will deliver more.

Deposit

It could be said that life brings you forward
when the basket of your experiences
needs to be deposited elsewhere.

Detour

Not every detour is intended to dampen your spirits. It's merely your character the universe wants to mold differently.

End

Ask the universe for the wide-open road, and
you get the narrow path to a dead end.

It's just a signpost, not the finish
line at the end of the race.

Flashlights

At what point does one recognize change?

When the flashlights cease, something's clearly amiss.

A noticeable shift. A habit beyond
its purpose has ended.

A standard calling card that went
beyond lighting the way.

Knowing the significance, its absence was plain.

It came time for someone else to gift
the flashlights for a change.

Frame

It's never too late to turn life around and frame a new picture on your wall of life.

Grief

Admit you are plunged in emotion while you pick up
the pieces and carry on. There is no success or failure
in this. Just be humble enough to welcome in grief.

Guide

Life takes our hands and walks us down
a path toward wisdom in hopes that she
does not have to take us back to our
starting points to walk the path again.

Hands

By design, you hold the future in your hand, and today is simply a milestone to remind you that you have two hands to grab wonder with.

Hitchhiker

Were we to hitch every opportunity to land with both feet on the ground, we might be disappointed. Not every leg of a trip sets us in motion.

The lags may be the rest stops that determine what lies ahead, stays behind, or is avoided altogether.

The road is not here simply to be traversed. You don't fail for making changes in the journey. Nor is the time clock in competition with the mile markers.

It's your life, unfolding as it may.

Instability

Not every firm grip on what's in front of you is stable. Look for the instability to offer opportunity rather than downfall.

Kiss

Sometimes you just have to grab life and
give it a big fat kiss so it'll take you seriously
enough to walk you farther down the aisle.

Leap

Leaping forward is something individuals are quite accustomed to doing. Ticking past one age to another must be child's play to one who reaches far beyond the backyard of youth.

Lemons

Prop a friend when he or she is downtrodden.
It's an eternity waiting for something to
squeeze through to the other side.

Holding a lemon is merely transition.
If you twist, what follows is better than planned.

Light

Even in disappointment, one finds the means to illuminate the way positively.

Loss

The hope of understanding is lost in the news
of death while in service, a stark reminder that
war abroad is not just a soldier's journey.

Those who wield words to tell the story are
just as vulnerable as those who are armed.

We are left holding their sacrifices in our
hands as citizens while our hearts ache
with the knowledge of their absence.

Measure

Measure a life-changing moment in
retrospect. It is the best reflection of just
how well you've managed to travel.

In the instant, it is rather indeterminable,
but once through to the other side, the
value of experience arrives on point.

Gauge failure, success, or the distance you've
traveled from origin to ascertain the present, but it's
where you find yourself standing that matters more.

Minute

Only the moment when life hands you another minute does it matter more.

Numbers

The time is not turning; nor are the numbers rising.
It's simply your presence on earth being
accounted for through celebration.

Ordinary

Common sense is a turn of phrase
for native good judgment.

Far more often, the lack of prudence captures our
attention. Or is it simply the harsh reality that living
reasonably and safely is no longer ordinary?

Prosper

A free world holds promise.

When each chance is certain to be rooted
in prosperity, the eye of the beholder sees
no barrier. The desire for something more
is ever present in the human condition.

These aspirations for success start early and
end late on an assembly line, the sweatshop
floor, or a migrating farm field.

These conditions reside closer to home as
the young discover the limits of an economy
squeezed by poor decision-making and baby
boomers find themselves expendable.

Such are the times we live in.

Reinvention

Continuing to reinvent yourself makes you
attractive. Being given another year in
life is a chance to smell the roses.

Remaining

Tucked away for safekeeping, habit, or neurosis, it's
hard to say at what point one enveloped the other.

The resulting clutter held meaning and order at
some juncture. Now it sits in an overwhelming
mix of decisions about what to keep, what
to share, and what to cast away.

It's less about what's left of one's life
and more about what remains.

Remembrance

Another year, here's another toast to you
without you here, giving you every reason to
laugh and smile from some kinder place.

Return

Returning strikes the same chord to emit a
familiar note. The change is only evident
in the instrument that gets played.

Time

Time passes, and we continue to reach
further into and outside of our true selves.
We frame questions with the knowledge that
the answers will come eventually. And many
times, it seems yesterday has yet to begin.

Vessel

We start this life as vessels to fill. We push through life filling other vessels, making a difference before we become obsolete. It's just what we vessels do.

Victory

Victory follows the notion that one must overcome some hurdle or obstacle. But it's really about pushing through to the end of the day and repeating the same day after day.

Walk

There's always celebration in our first steps. Later we woefully mourn no longer traversing in an ebullient fashion. In between, we move, we fall, we teeter, we totter, we step backward, and we even walk in place, but it still gets us here or there.

Year

Not every year can be the same; nor can every year go as we planned. The surest thing is that we are provided another year, every year, to make life grand.

PART 2

COMMUNITY

Alive

What brings health and wealth to every human
being can be found in his or her ability to stay in the
stream, surrounded by every element of happiness.

Beauty

So much can be said of beauty. It is visual,
experiential, and appreciated by all.

Natural vistas thrive in plain sight, and yet
some remain vigilant to clip it as adornment
to wither in some interior landscape.

Were sabbaticals not intended to
make us pause and take in?

Fabricate those climes, and it is short-lived. Step out
into it, and sense the realness of what was intended.

Witness charm and splendor rather
than settle for it secondhand.

Bonds

Extraordinary are the strands that bind. Hearts and minds understand the draw even when the odds play a different hand in the distance in between.

The endurance linking each hand across the table is a testament to the reach. Somewhere beyond familiar and hidden from public view, but very much in play, it's never really folding.

Bridges

Bridges between places and people, however causal, tether you in a moment, near or far.

Capacity

While humans have great capacity, it is
just that, the capacity to open and fill our
lives in ways that make a difference to us
individually as well as to others collectively.

Some choose to limit their capacities, while
others elect to extend their potential.

One need only look to the many stars above and as
many universes beyond to know that there is far more
space than we mere mortals can fill here on earth.

Clock

Triggered by a phrase and inspired by a
notion, the wafting aroma of familiarity echoes
along the passage of a time stamp.

Placing memory in present tense is a
hobby of our internal clocks.

Grasping these elements, our
second hand winds round.

Commitment

Commitment to the moment in which you find yourself in is far more virtuous than the inability to commit to the green, grassy lawn you are wallowing in.

Compass

Love and compassion lay plain the arc of our
being. Challenged only by convention and
narrow thinking, they blossom many times over.

Like much of what we humans face, the connection
with grace simply glides us past turbulent seas.
We experience them and live through them
but always land on the other side of them.

Is the journey plotted by a compass or
charted in maps? Perhaps, but even maps
age, and compasses lose their direction.

Concoction

Ripe with newness accompanied by the
comfort of the familiar, a concoction is poured
for the soul and consumed as needed.

Connect

The sum total of experience is but a fraction
of what may be discovered on the surface;
however, it always connects us to others.

Dads

Some fathers are related to us;
others just find their way to us.

Just being there knowing they stand
with us makes us strong.

Debate

Debating the responsible party for what
appears outdated and attacked for what it
lacks. That which digresses from the holy
rail is smeared for what it discounts.

The questions raised from deliberate points
of reference seem a likely battleground
for what there is in common. Living is for
an individual to choose purposefully.

That does not require a consensus,
merely acceptance.

December

What's not to love about a month of stealing kisses under mistletoe, spending time in the kitchen making nog and ramping up the naughty or nice meter?

There are elves that do more than sit on shelves.

Dining

A wait brines what is served, much like
a puppeteer plays the stage.

Never lacking charm or wit, we ever work against
becoming obsolete by stringing along the naves.
Awash in the language of pleasantries, we
balance a myriad of demands and preferences
ever accompanied by fits of exhaustion.

It's a life made whole by seats occupied with hungry
people and spare change left on tabletops.

Expectations

A family blended by time and circumstance
may not visibly appear any different from the
usual structure, but the nuances of individual
expectations require a new foundation.

Friends

The far side of disappointment finds joy in other
surroundings. While others elect to benchmark
life in past tense, the choice of a future with
far more gain becomes the obvious choice.

Causalities are the individuals lacking the
foresight, the glean of something better.
It's best to let go the hope they'll come
around one day. Such odds are not favored.

It's better to plant where thriving equates
with nurturing aspirations with love.
Those fields prosper by friendships built to last.

Generosity

Money can, in times when it is not plentiful, create selfish acts of preservation rather than generosity.

Be generous, and everyone is rich.

Merry

Make merry, love boldly, and find time for family
and friends as we flow through this holiday
toward the end of the year. Give your thoughts
to those who lives may need some cheer.
Near or far, your kindness is always the shining star.

Mothering

Mothering has a place in every heart,
those that bring it to their own or others.

Tenderness by any hand brings
our best selves forward.

Honor them. Love ourselves.

Optimism

During a time when everyone carried eternal optimism with them, people were light on their feet, weighted only by a few burdens, and literally everything was in motion.

Overlook

Zoom in to maximize that view. Up close
and personal improves your position but may
overlook the very scene you wish to capture.

Place

A physical place may shift and bend with the
changing times and trends, but the essence of what
makes it wholly a place to return to remains the same.

A place is one can always call home
even after life pulls you away.

Rich

The day you forged your way in and the way you continue to make a difference makes us all rich.

Scales

Balance the hours of time well spent
with the demands of your trade.

Happy are they who love what they do. It is true.

Counterbalanced, a level playing field between, is
the ideal. More often than not, the only meaning
worth measuring is how often one tips the scales.

Share

Share what you can when you and steal
away any minute that makes that possible.
In the communion of figurative space, times
get lost, and meaning translates.

Slip

You are as close as an invitation and only as far away as you let time slip by.

Three

Things grouped by three, make of these as you please, and know that, while things are aglow above us and below, every twinkle and spark is a reminder of the grace and fellowship we share.

Together

For what we have in gift and friend, there is no greater joy than to simply be together this day and as many days as we can join together.

Trenches

Never tire in the trenches, as that is
where hearty people reside.

Unencumbered

Invariably humans extend invitations and
retreat from them throughout life.

Knowing which offer holds the most promise
whilst a host of opportunities stream ahead
can be quite daunting for those encumbered
with the worry of making mistakes.

Mistakes improve one's position to recognize fortune.

United

Bully the individual who appears to stand in
isolation, and you just might find an armored
mass equally charged to wave the flag higher.

Visualize

The best way to visualize the body of water
called life is as an archipelago. Many isolated
islands are connected by association.

PART 3

DISCOURSE

Boldness

Speaking frankly in a pretentious world can wreak havoc. No matter how charming one may be, you are breaking the code of the backslapping brethren. Who really wants their back slapped when it's the face of man's dignity that needs resurrected?

Collective

The beauty of scholarly or literary work is
to provide the collective with an opportunity
to frame an independent point of view.

Compliments

Always be inspired by a compliment, even
the ones that simply evaluate the outer
view of your world. Sometimes it takes a
brain to inspire others to look inward.

Conversation

Some things are best thrown away to rot elsewhere when the conversation is laden with stench. Great depth and smoldering personality do not always win.

Drown

Points of view polarized by ideas eventually drown each other in dogma, leaving nothing but the memory of discourse behind it.

Engage

Deplorable table service, children underserved,
and the absence of engagement, each represents
the critical gap between success and failure.

The expectation that some ideal state manifests
without the benefit of interaction is in itself regressive.
Far better are we to play the proactive part than to
project reactionary displeasure at what we distain.

Evaluate

The most valuable part of life is not delivered in a neat and tidy package. Instead look to the crushing moment of disappointment or the sidesplitting roar of laughter to reach higher.

Far

In a lifetime of chance, longing cast across a
room may find its spring. Removed from present
tense, it lingers in the deep-set eyes of war.

Connected by simple notions amid a
great many disturbances, the permanence
of which is brief, yet enduring.

Were it possible to discover the essence
of what could be, one may be just as
close as one is far, but known.

Ilk

What is not seen is heard in the resounding realization that the rug has been pulled out from under your feet. You are now standing outside, looking back at a closed door, one you had walked through for an eternity, never expecting to lose entry.

The opportunity should be obvious. Spend greater hours in the company of the thoughtful and kind or stare at a closed door whose countenance is unwaveringly bewitched by an intrepid sort.

With no regrets, follow a choice to walk away from the ilk and go through doors that swing wide open.

Influence

Ubiquitous is influence. What we find everywhere
may not serve to fulfill our knowledge quest; nor
should we allow it to frack the environment around us.

Juncture

Hands placed on the hips takes a stance when
solo but carries a wholly different meaning when
another cusps them in an embrace. A single
gesture brings measure to the emotion at hand.

Leadership

People are who they are. It's best to
choose the path that makes the most
sense to accomplish what is at hand.

Transparency keeps people and aims
aligned. Anything else is ego-driven
mania not intended to coalesce.

Leadership contrived by physique and
photo ops building dialogue around what
others lack isn't leading, merely an autocrat
dangling diplomas without substance.

Name

Never is a moment grander than the one that welcomed you into this world and gave you a name.

Peace

What one day brings in memory, we rally in spirit
as a diverse nation proud to know her people.

The loss, the grieving, and the courage are the
elements from which we find unity to see our future.

Today is an anniversary on which
we each rest hope for peace.

Privacy

Privacy is the proverbial sliding scale of comfort and discomfort that does not end but trails onward. What sensationalized Vincent van Gogh in painting his own image was a herald to the modern-day selfie.

Quiet

Quiet time spent in contemplation places
one on the path in front of him or her.
Avoiding silence is a detour.

Remove

To lose an article of personal relevance
involves the unintentional act of misplacing it,
but to purposefully remove it without discourse
is a travesty under any circumstance.

Rites

When the last rite takes the sharpest turn from
telling the story true, we must see beyond the
walls of structured halls to set spirits free or simply
die in the lie of some shrouded rhapsody.

Roots

I've not always been faithful when the lure of
prospects elsewhere seemed far more appealing.
I did and do digress. Yet here I am rooted in a
way of life bound to meet some end well.

Silence

Rendered speechless with a great deal to
say, silence brings company in the manner of
listening during still moments like these.

Purpose exists in retreats from the conversation, the
hum, the charade of life playing out in sound.

Hearing your own heart beat just might be the
best speaking engagement you've ever had.

Storytelling

Life is never ending as long as there is a story to tell. A heart full of memories to share leaves a life in the hands of others to tell.

Streets

Street life in urban areas bellows several stories
up, a constant hum with genuine purpose.

At some point, silence eclipses the cackle
of conversations, vehicles rolling over
sewer covers and bus stop requiems.

Slumber is short-lived. Living resounds
loudly regardless of the hour.

Swing

Miss the point or the points in
between, and we swing away.

Nothing is strange as long as
you know who's batting.

Travel

Travel between two points long enough, and the road between no longer seems like a journey, the surest sign it is time to change up the commute.

Tribute

A tribute to one of the finest sort is what is worn through the ages, remaining timeless yet in tune with each reflection of grace.

Trust

Trust, like the effort, will never fail, even
when common sense says otherwise.
Many times the reliability one seeks is not
in an act but found in a notion of faith.

Blindly we frame our words around honesty,
assuring those closest that they must first accept the
claim before truth will render. As such, making a
staunch conviction necessary to grab the intent.

Understandably some stay silent.

Understand

Understanding does not come by demanding
it or confining it to some far-removed
standard. It flourishes where acceptance
allows for difference ... and not until then.

Wit

One must seek out mirth and joy to envelop
it in. Gladness and gaiety are not rare
occurrences; nor are they ever in short supply.

Jollity in its singular context is but an individual's
capacity to make merry. Plural, it tends to be far more
festive, amplified by volume, an occasion elevated.
It bubbles up and floats, making all else fade away.

About the Author

Ann-Marie Adams loves words, written and spoken. *Word Strings* is Ms. Adams' second creative collection. Her first endeavor, *Aquabet* reimagines the letters of the American alphabet as sea creatures. She is a natural storyteller with nearly two decades of experience in public engagement. Her academic pursuits in strategic communication are focused on the evolution of discourse in a multi-mobile environment.

Currently Ann-Marie splits her time between the Lowcountry region of South Carolina, the Finger Lakes region of New York, and East Tennessee to teach, write, and porch sit.